Super Smart Animals

Dogs
Are Smart!

Leigh Rockwood

PowerKiDS press

New York

Published in 2010 by The Rosen Publishing Group, Inc.
29 East 21st Street, New York, NY 10010

First Edition

Editor: Amelie von Zumbusch
Book Design: Julio Gil
Photo Researcher: Jessica Gerweck

Photo Credits: Cover, back cover (dog) courtesy of Lindsy Whitten; back cover (chimpanzee) Manoj Shah/ Getty Images; back cover (dolphin, horse, parrot, pig), pp. 6, 9, 10, 13, 14, 21 Shutterstock.com; p. 5 Ariel Skelley/Getty Images; p. 17 Peter Lilja/Getty Images; p. 18 Altrendo Images/Getty Images.

Library of Congress Cataloging-in-Publication Data

Rockwood, Leigh.
  Dogs are smart! / Leigh Rockwood. — 1st ed.
     p. cm. — (Super smart animals)
  Includes index.
  ISBN 978-1-4358-9374-0 (library binding) — ISBN 978-1-4358-9836-3 (pbk.) — ISBN 978-1-4358-9837-0 (6-pack)
  1. Dogs—Juvenile literature. 2. Dogs—Psychology—Juvenile literature. I. Title.
  SF426.5.R615 2010
  636.7—dc22
                                                2009031758

Manufactured in the United States of America

CPSIA Compliance Information: Batch #WW10PK: For Further Information contact Rosen Publishing, New York, New York at 1-800-237-9932

Contents

Man's Smart Friend

People have kept dogs as pets throughout history. In fact, people **domesticated** dogs from wolves over 10,000 years ago. Although you might think of dogs as family pets, people also train dogs to work with them as hunters and herders. Dogs guard people's homes and farm animals, too. There are even dogs that have saved people's lives!

Dogs have been able to do all of this for people because they are smart. As people do, dogs need to learn new things to keep from getting bored. These smart animals can do great things when they put their minds to it!

This boy is playing with his dog. Dogs are well-liked pets. About two out of every five Americans has a dog for a pet. ▶

Dogs and Their Senses

Dogs are four-legged **mammals**. Dogs are a single **species**, but within this species are hundreds of **breeds**. This huge number of breeds is why dogs come in many shapes and sizes. For example, Chihuahuas weigh only a few pounds (kg), while Great Danes can weigh more than 150 pounds (70 kg).

Dogs have better senses of smell and hearing than people do. They can smell and hear things that are faint or far away. These senses make dogs great at finding things people cannot. This is why people use dogs when searching for things like lost people or hidden drugs.

◀ **This dog is a husky. Like many dogs, huskies have such an excellent sense of smell that they can sense animals under the snow.**

So Many Breeds

There are around 400 different dog breeds in the world! The reason there are so many is because dogs have been **bred** for many different jobs and **temperaments**. For example, Jack Russell terriers were first bred to hunt small animals. Huskies were bred to be sledding dogs.

While dogs can be trained, each breed has some natural behaviors, or ways of acting. A pug would be bad at herding sheep, and a Border collie would be unhappy sitting quietly in a small apartment. This is important to think about when you are choosing a dog for a pet.

These small dogs are Chihuahuas. Chihuahuas are the smallest breed of dog. They generally weigh less than 6 pounds (3 kg). ▶

Dog Talk

Dogs are **omnivores**. Dog food is often made of grains, such as corn and rice, and meats, such as beef and chicken. Dogs sometimes beg for their owners' food. However, some foods that people eat, such as chocolate and onions, are harmful or deadly to dogs.

Dogs **communicate** with barks, howls, and growls, as well as with their bodies. Wagging their tails, flattening their ears, or laying belly up on the ground are some of the ways dogs communicate their moods to each other and to people. For example, a dog with a **relaxed** body and a wagging tail is usually feeling playful and calm.

◄ When a dog snarls, or shows its teeth, it is telling others to stay away. When a dog narrows its eyes, that is also a sign to keep away.

Growing Pups

Male and female dogs reach adulthood between one and two years of age, depending on their breed. Adult dogs are able to **mate**. About two months after mating, females give birth to a litter of puppies. A litter can have between three and nine puppies.

Puppies learn by watching their mother and by playing with each other. At around two months old, puppies are ready to begin **socialization**. Socialization helps puppies feel confident and learn the behavioral training they need. Well-cared-for, healthy dogs often live between 12 and 15 years. Dogs from small breeds generally live longer than dogs from larger breeds.

Puppies, such as these young dogs, grow a lot in their first few weeks. At between two and three weeks old, their eyes and ears open and they begin to walk. ▶

How Smart Are Dogs?

It is hard to measure a dog's intelligence against that of other animals. Scientists who study dogs measure how quickly dogs learn new tasks, or jobs. They also note how many tasks dogs remember. For example, a Border collie named Rico learned the names of 200 different objects and quickly learned new ones.

Scientists think that super smart dogs like Rico learn new words in the same way that people do as babies. They also think that this kind of learning is something that has grown out of dogs' living closely with people. The scientists believe that wolves could not learn to do this.

◀ **This dog is a Border collie. Most people who study dogs think that Border collies are the smartest breed of dog.**

Hardworking Dogs

Some types of working dogs have been bred for their jobs. They have a natural talent for their work, and they have been trained to follow people's commands. Border collies were bred to herd cows, goats, and sheep. Though herding animals by circling and barking at them comes naturally to Border collies, farmers must still teach the dogs their commands for directing the herd.

Siberian huskies were bred to pull sleds over ice and snow. They have thick fur to keep warm and are strong for their size. Large teams of sled dogs have even been able to move a bus!

This team of dogs is pulling a sled in northern Sweden. People have used dog sleds to get around in the Far North for hundreds of years. ▶

Service Dogs

Service dogs are taught to help people. They learn special skills that make use of their intelligence, patience, or senses of hearing and smell. Service dogs are trained from puppyhood. The dogs are often put to work after about a year of training. German shepherds and golden retrievers are two of the breeds most commonly used as service dogs.

Guide dogs help people who are blind or **disabled** get around safely. Police dogs are taught to sniff, or smell, out drugs or bombs. Search and rescue dogs can find someone who became lost in the wilderness by following that person's scent, or smell.

◀ **Guide dogs, such as the one seen here, often wear a harness. The dog's handler, or owner, holds on to the harness.**

Dog Training

Dogs need training to be well-behaved family members. Important behavioral commands are "sit," "stay," "come," and "heel." "Fetch" and "roll over" are two tricks that are easy to teach most dogs.

Dogs naturally live in groups called packs. Dogs almost always follow the commands of their pack leaders. When you are training a dog, that dog needs to know that you are its leader. People training dogs need to be clear which behaviors are good and which are bad, so that dogs can learn what to do. Praise and treats for correct tricks or good behavior tend to be the best way to teach dogs.

You must be firm with a dog when you are training it. Many dog owners use both speech and hand movements to tell their dogs what to do.

21

Strong Bonds

Since they were first domesticated, dogs have formed strong bonds with people. Dogs are known for being loyal, or true, to their owners. People and dogs can find great joy in each other's company. In fact, dogs are sometimes known as man's best friend.

Over the past few years, their friendliness has led to yet another job for dogs. **Therapy** dogs are service dogs that are brought to hospitals and nursing homes for patients to pet. Doctors have found that petting the dogs improves peoples' moods, which often helps them heal faster. That is certainly something to wag a tail about!

Glossary

bred (BRED) To have brought a male and a female animal together so they will have babies.

breeds (BREEDZ) Groups of animals that look alike and have the same relatives.

communicate (kuh-MYOO-nih-kayt) To share facts or feelings.

disabled (dis-AY-beld) Unable to do certain things.

domesticated (duh-MES-tih-kayt-id) Raised to live with people.

mammals (MA-mulz) Warm-blooded animals that have backbones and hair, breathe air, and feed milk to their young.

mate (MAYT) To come together to make babies.

omnivores (OM-nih-vorz) Animals that eat both plants and animals.

relaxed (ree-LAKSD) Free of tightness, nervousness, or worry.

socialization (soh-shuh-luh-ZAY-shun) Learning to be friendly.

species (SPEE-sheez) One kind of living thing. All people are one species.

temperaments (TEM-pur-ments) Characters or natures.

therapy (THER-uh-pee) Having to do with the treatment of health problems.

Index

B
body, 11
breed(s), 7–8, 12, 19

C
Chihuahuas, 7

D
drugs, 7, 19

G
Great Danes, 7

H
herders, 4

history, 4
homes, 4, 22
hospitals, 22
hunters, 4

J
Jack Russell terriers, 8
job(s), 8, 15–16, 22

M
mammals, 7

O
omnivores, 11

P
pet(s), 4, 8, 22

S
senses, 7, 19
shapes, 7
size(s), 7, 16
socialization, 12
species, 7

T
temperaments, 8

W
wolves, 4, 15

Web Sites

Due to the changing nature of Internet links, PowerKids Press has developed an online list of Web sites related to the subject of this book. This site is updated regularly. Please use this link to access the list: www.powerkidslinks.com/ssan/dog/